ZAPiRO
Hasta la Gupta, baby!

Cartoons from *Daily•Maverick, Sunday Times, Mail & Guardian, The Times*

JACANA

Acknowledgements: Thanks to my editors at the Sunday Times (Bongani Siqoko, S'Thembiso Msomi) and at The Times (Stephen Haw, Dominic Mahlangu); thanks to my Mail & Guardian editors (Khadija Patel, Shaun de Waal and the many brilliant editors I worked under for 23 years); special thanks to my new editors at Daily Maverick (Branko Brkic and Marianne Thamm for their ideas and passion and for giving me a front row seat to history); thanks to the production staff at all the newspapers and online; thanks to Mike Wills for again writing captions and whipping me past the finishing post; to Richard Hainebach for continuing to manage my website, ePublications and publishing rights; special thanks to my assistant Eleanora Bresler for holding even more together; Roberto Millan for more masterful cover colour; Bridget Impey, Russell Martin, Nadia Goetham, Janine Daniel and all at Jacana; Claudine Willatt-Bate yet again for layout; at home, Nomalizo Ndlazi and my family, Karina, Tevya and Nina, for their constant love and support. Oh, and thanks JZ for the shower, Donald Trump for the golden version and Brian Molefe for the Saxonwold Shebeen.

10 Orange Street
Sunnyside
Auckland Park 2092
South Africa
(+27 11) 628 3200
www.jacana.co.za

in association with

PRODUCTIONS

ISBN 978-1-4314-2575-4

Cover design by Jonathan Shapiro

Page layout by Claudine Willatt-Bate
Printed and bound by ABC Press, Cape Town
Job no. 003117

See a complete list of Jacana titles at www.jacana.co.za

See Zapiro's list and archive at www.zapiro.com

for maverick writers, fight the good fighters,
hypocrisy haters, sabc eighters,
fake news detectors, real public protectors,
for dirt diggers and go figures,
truth to power speakers and gupta leakers

ZAPIRO annuals

The Madiba Years (1996)
The Hole Truth (1997)
End of Part One (1998)
Call Mr Delivery (1999)
The Devil Made Me Do It! (2000)
The ANC Went in 4x4 (2001)
Bushwhacked (2002)
Dr Do-Little and the African Potato (2003)
Long Walk to Free Time (2004)
Is There a Spin Doctor In the House? (2005)
Da Zuma Code (2006)
Take Two Veg and Call Me In the Morning (2007)
Pirates of Polokwane (2008)
Don't Mess With the President's Head (2009)
Do You Know Who I Am?! (2010)
The Last Sushi (2011)
But Will It Stand Up In Court? (2012)
My Big Fat Gupta Wedding (2013)
It's Code Red! (2014)
Rhodes Rage (2015)
Dead President Walking (2016)

Other books

The Mandela Files (2008)
VuvuzelaNation (2013)
DemoCrazy (2014)

19 October 2016   Samsung has an exploding smartphone problem

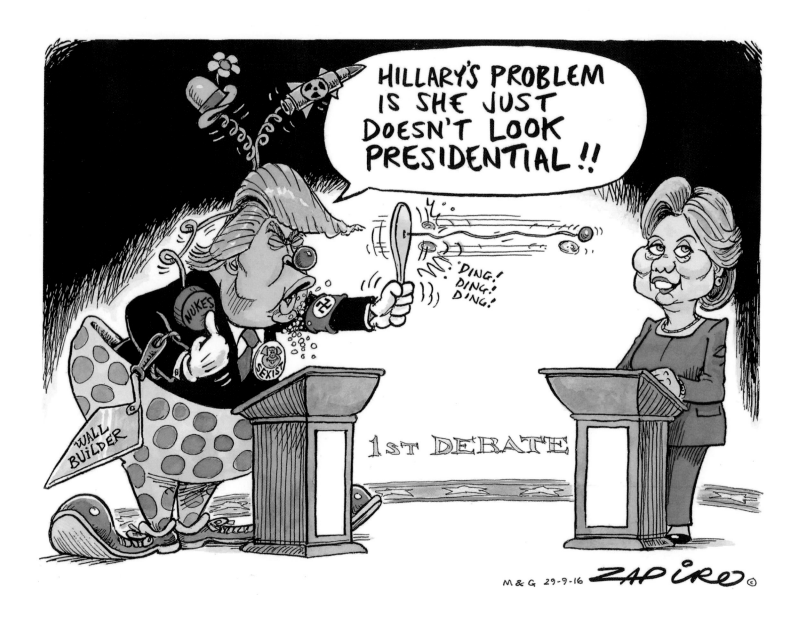

29 September 2016

Donald Trump – misogynist, bigot and liar –
criticises his election opponent's appearance

SA PROTECTED SPECIES

RHINO — POACHED FOR HORN

PANGOLIN — POACHED FOR MEAT AND SCALES

ELEPHANT — POACHED FOR IVORY

HLAUDI — USELESS NOISY PEST, NO VALID REASON FOR PROTECTION

COP 17 CITES WORLD WILDLIFE CONFERENCE JO'BURG 2016

ZAPIRO SUN. TIMES 2·10·16

Global environmentalists gather in SA while the SABC board plans to reinstate unqualified COO Hlaudi Motsoeneng in spite of a highly critical Public Protector's report and multiple court rulings against him

2 October 2016

OFFICE OF THE PUBLIC PROTECTOR

'95–'02
BAQWA

'02–'09
MUSHWANA

'09–'16
MADONSELA

2016–2023
MKHWEBANE

ANN7
GUPTA TV

State Capture Report

THULI'S PROGRESS

23-10-16
SUN.TIMES
ZAPIRO

...AND JUST LIKE THAT, ORDER IS RESTORED!

23 October 2016

The new Public Protector denigrates her stellar predecessor and won't oppose
President Zuma's move to block the release of Madonsela's report on state capture

8

PARTY WHIP

ZAPIRO
THE TIMES 25-10-16

ANC chief whip Jackson Mthembu backs beleaguered
finance minister Pravin Gordhan, urges colleagues to speak out
and questions whether the entire party leadership is fit and proper

25 October 2016

27 October 2016

No-nonsense finance minister Pravin Gordhan tackles the economic crisis
as he faces trumped-up fraud charges from NPA boss Shaun Abrahams

10

28 October 2016

In an obvious charade, President Zuma says Gordhan is innocent
until proven guilty and the law must be allowed to take its course

1 November 2016   Humiliating back-pedal for Abrahams as he withdraws charges against Gordhan

Pretoria High Court orders long-delayed release of the damning
report implicating Zuma and family members, parastatal execs
and the main players – brothers Ajay, Atul and Rajesh Gupta

3 November 2016

14

4 November 2016

6 November 2016

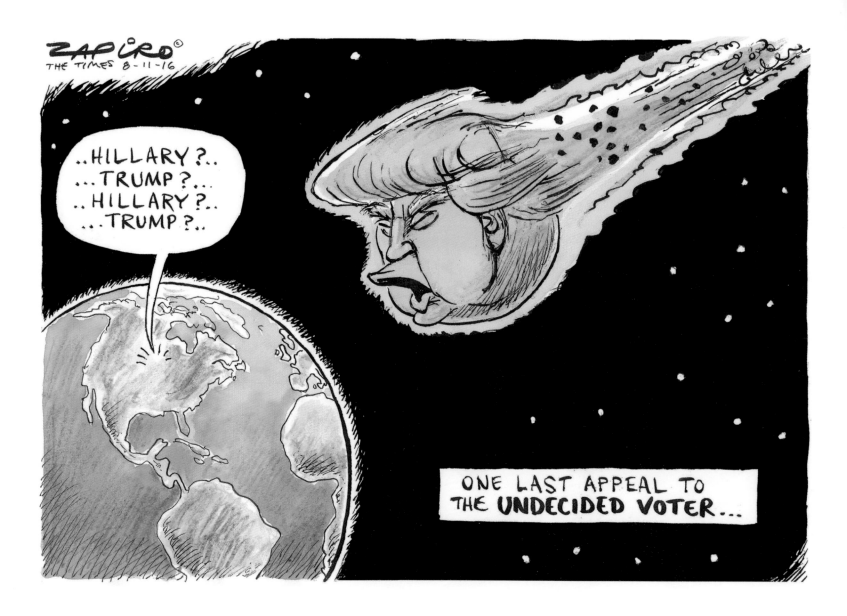

9 November 2016

State Capture report ties Eskom CEO Brian Molefe to the Gupta mansion through traced cellphone records. He tearfully resigns and claims his many recorded visits to the upmarket Saxonwold, where the brothers live, may have been to a mysterious shebeen — which no journalist can find.

13 November 2016

15 November 2016

Al Jazeera report links state security minister David Mahlobo to
Guan Jiang Guang, a rhino horn trafficker and Mbombela massage parlour owner

DEAD AND BURIED?

Verwoerd

APARTHATE

M&G 18-11-16

ZAPIRO

18 November 2016

Two Middelburg men face serious charges after their own YouTube video shows them forcing a farmworker into a coffin and threatening to kill him

Bok skipper Adriaan Strauss says they've hit rock bottom
after first-ever loss to Italy. Proteas' skipper Faf du Plessis
is accused of ball tampering during test triumph in Australia.

22 November 2016

24 November 2016

Limpopo pastor sprays Doom insect repellent over his congregation to 'heal' them. ANC stalwarts back down from a challenge to Zuma's leadership.

25

29 November 2016

ANC executive committee considers Zuma's fate

1 December 2016

Divisions reported within NEC but somehow he survives again

25 November 2016   American crazy sales day tradition hits SA big time

6 December 2016

Surprising upset in West African ballot

9 December 2016

Marking Zuma's disastrous decision to fire finance minister
Nhlanhla Nene and replace him with Des van Rooyen

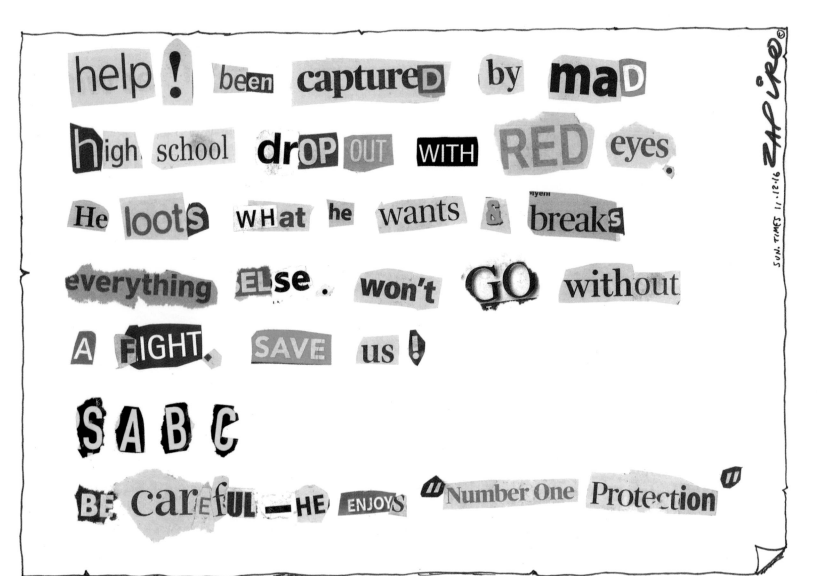

11 December 2016   SABC staff fear retribution for revealing more corrupt craziness under Hlaudi Motsoeneng

13 December 2016   Western Cape High Court rules Motsoeneng's appointment was unlawful

OUTLANDISH WORKS OF FANTASY

15 December 2016

Zuma's hatchet men at the Hawks lay a preposterous string of
charges against known opponents including IPID boss Robert McBride,
private investigator Paul O'Sullivan and former Gauteng Hawks head Shadrack Sibiya

18 December 2016

Freak storm destroys a marquee the moment the president
mentions the 2012 Marikana massacre of 34 miners by police

2016 FESTIVE DRONE DELIVERIES

22 December 2016

My final cartoon for *Mail & Guardian* after 23 years

23 December 2016

Mired in controversy, Zuma tells an ANC Youth League rally that he'll never resign on his own because that would be surrendering to monopoly capital

ANC secretary general Gwede Mantashe bemoans factionalism.
As if no one's noticed the race that's already well under way.

12 January 2017

38

13 January 2017

Washington's new administration

15 January 2017

Now it's Ford with a crisis as Kuga SUVs catch fire

SHOWER HEAD | **GOLDEN SHOWER HEAD**

17 January 2017

Explosive, unverified allegations that Russians have
dirt on Trump including some strange sexual preferences

41

20 January 2017

No big names are prepared to perform for him

21 January 2017   Inaugural fake news – the president and his spokesman claim the biggest crowd ever

Orchestrated media campaign targets the finance minister

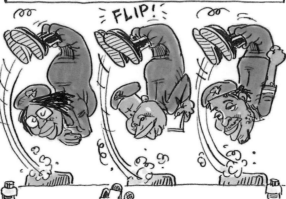

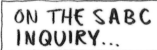

EFF holds third plenum and changes its mind on many points

26 January 2017

ANC spokesman denies party sanctioned 'war room' running covert social media campaigns that falsely maligned opposition parties during the municipal elections

In a suspicious contradiction of previous inquiries, the Public Protector rules that ABSA (one of many banks refusing to hold Gupta-connected accounts) should pay billions for an apartheid-era bailout. Gupta mouthpiece Collen Maine threatens Youth League mass action.

29 January 2017

31 January 2017

Trump executive order suspends refugee admissions and
bans entry by anyone from seven Muslim-majority nations

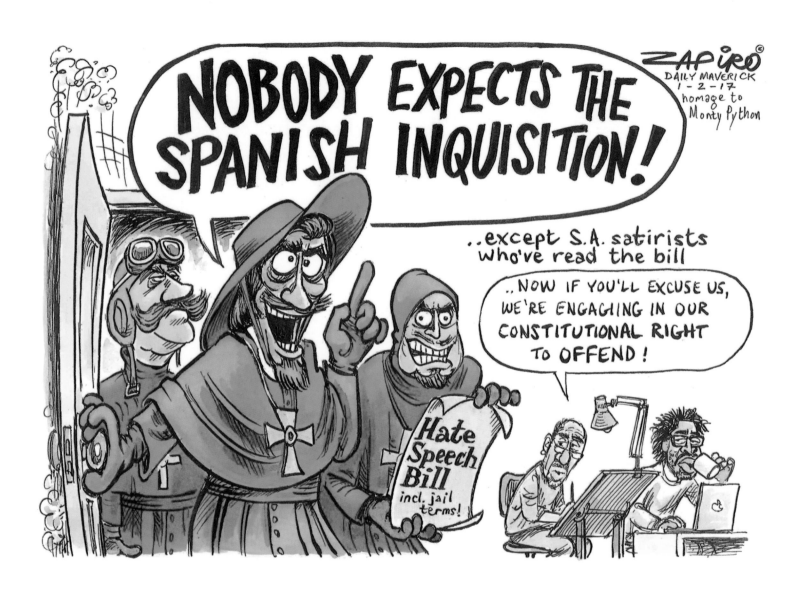

1 February 2017

The ANC is pushing punitive and censorious
Prevention and Combating of Hate Crimes and Hate Speech Bill

2 February 2017

Slating selective prosecutions, the man who nailed Oscar
quits the NPA and joins civil society action group

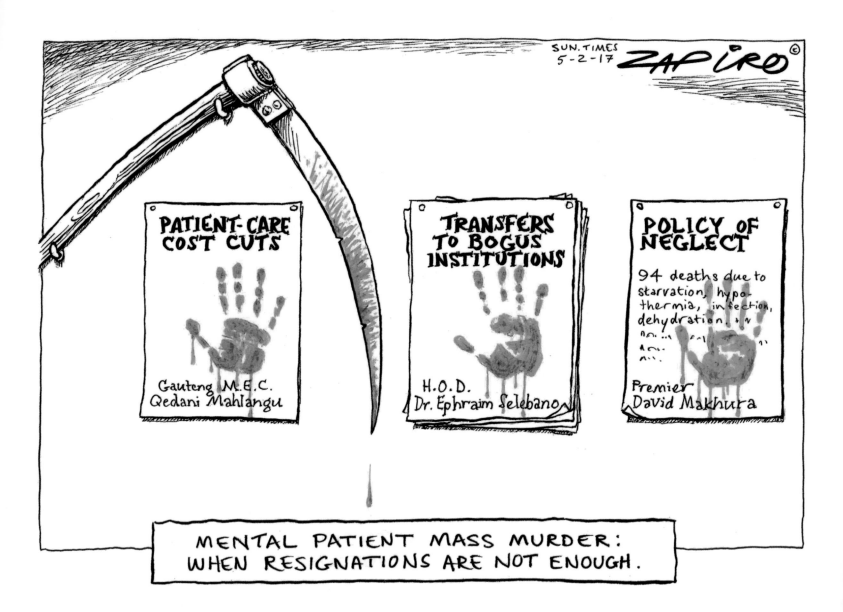

National health ombudsman reports shocking details of deaths of 94 mentally ill patients in Gauteng after transfers to unlicensed facilities … and of lies officials told his inquiry

5 February 2017

7 February 2017

44-year-old Springbok rugby icon Joost van der Westhuizen
widely mourned after losing a long battle with motor neuron disease

Ahead of the president's State of the Nation address, extra SANDF members,
riot police and parliamentary security are deployed to maintain order

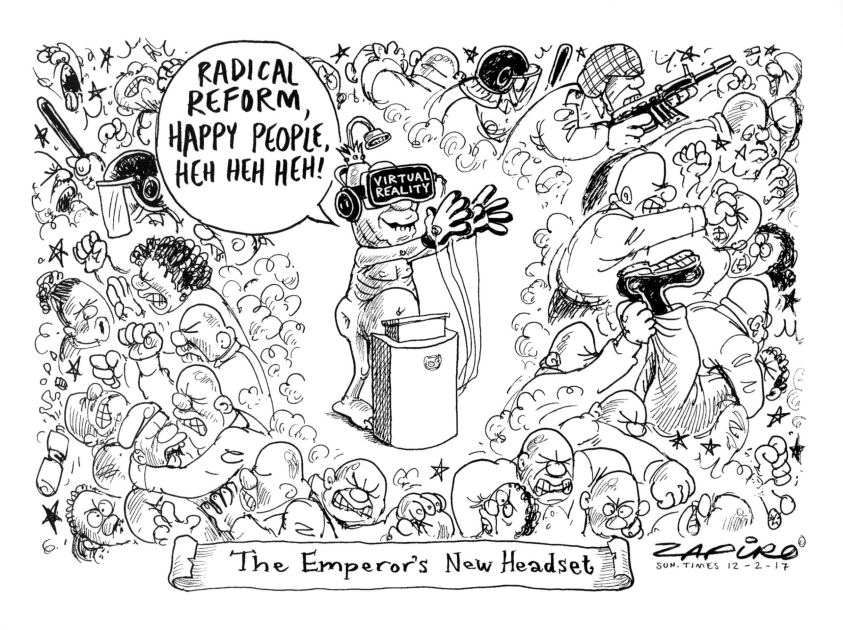

The Emperor's New Headset

12 February 2017

Chaos in parliament. EFF violently removed and
DA walks out before Zuma's bland speech can begin.

9 February 2017

TELECONFERENCE

14 February 2017

Presidents Zuma and Trump have their first chat

Private investigator and thorn in the side of corrupt cops, Paul O'Sullivan,
is arrested on orders of acting national police commissioner Khomotso Phahlane

16 February 2017

Competition Commission head Thembinkosi Bonakele refers ABSA, Standard, Investec and some foreign banks to the Competition Tribunal for price fixing

19 February 2017

21 February 2017

Out of Eskom, Molefe is hastily deployed to parliament just
before budget day. The word is he's lined up for Pravin Gordhan's job.

26 February 2017

Molefe will be sworn in today

NORTH WEST GOVT. TO ERECT 6m BRONZE ZUMA STATUE

GROOT MARICO

DROUGHT RESTRICTED

J.Z.

MARIKANA

ZAPIRO
DAILY MAVERICK
22-2-17

22 February 2017

Provincial premier Supra Mahumapelo proposes a monument
to the president at Groot Marico near Rustenburg

The grants payment system heads for a massive crisis as the social development minister blocks proper solutions and ignores the courts in favour of private contractors

23 February 2017

SOCIAL GRANTS CRISIS

Q. What are the chances of payment by month's end?

A. 17 million : one

DAILY MAVERICK 2·3·17 ZAPIRO ©

She fails to account to a parliamentary standing committee

First they came for the gays, and I did not speak out because I was not gay.

Then they came for the foreigners and I didn't speak out because I wasn't a foreigner.

UN-AFRICAN!

Then they came for the Agents of White Monopoly Capital and I didn't speak out because I wasn't one of them ... (I hoped?)

PRAVIN IMPIMPI!

By the time they came for me, Zuma/Trump alternative facts populism had screwed things up so much that no-one knew or cared.

& Apology to Pastor Niemöller
1-3-17 DAILY MAVERICK   ZAPIRO ©

1 March 2017

7 March 2017

Now a global high-flyer, local comic cracks a famous magazine cover

9 March 2017

State security minister David Mahlobo says government
wants to regulate social media to 'counter false narratives'

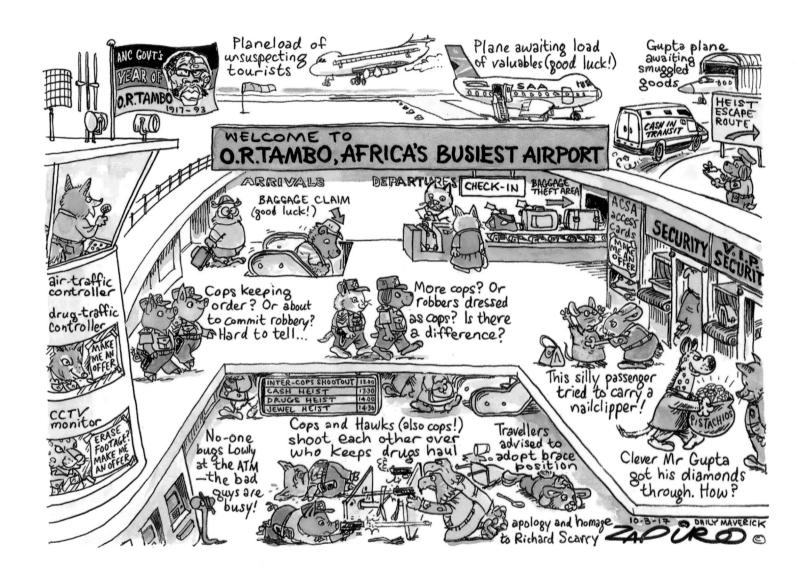

10 March 2017

A R200m cash heist and the Guptas reportedly blocked from taking a suitcase full of diamonds out of the country through an Oppenheimer-operated private terminal facility are just the latest stories out of Jo'burg's airport

12 March 2017

Those behind dodgy dealings at the passenger railways are not
on the PRASA board which the transport minister dissolves

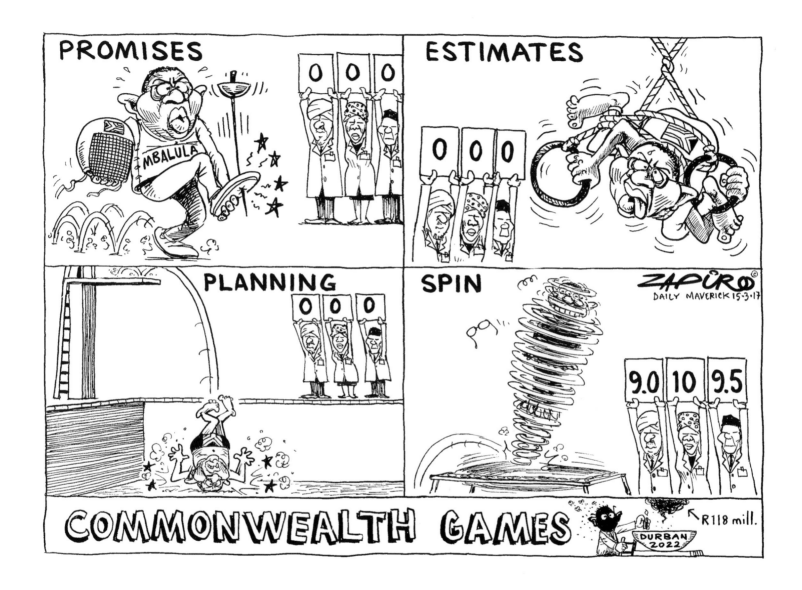

It's been big talk as usual from the sport and recreation minister Fikile Mbalula but Durban loses previously awarded hosting rights for the 2022 Commonwealth Games

16 March 2017

Social development minister Bathabile Dlamini defies the Constitutional Court and places 11 million grant recipients at risk. The court had ordered her to replace an illegal grants payment contract which she's hell-bent on extending as the deadline looms.

Yet more Twitter trouble for Western Cape premier Helen Zille whose
tweet from Singapore about the benefits of colonialism sparks
a furore and an investigation by DA leader Mmusi Maimane

19 March 2017

26 March 2017

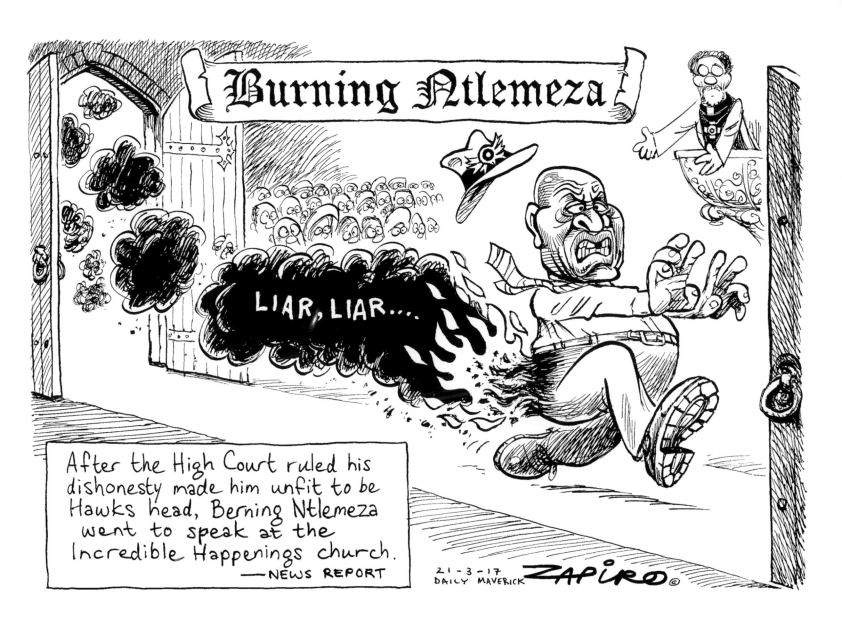

Burning Ntlemeza

LIAR, LIAR....

After the High Court ruled his dishonesty made him unfit to be Hawks head, Berning Ntlemeza went to speak at the Incredible Happenings church.
— NEWS REPORT

21-3-17
DAILY MAVERICK
ZAPIRO ©

21 March 2017

day	day	day	day	
6 Marikana Massacre inaction day	**7** Screw 17 million social grantees day	**8** Esidimeni no arrests day	**9** Use millions meant for the poor day	**10**
13 Cash for tenders day	**14** Smear media and whistleblowers day	**15** Use captured state organ to hide evidence day	**16** Reshuffle non-delivering Cabinet cronies day	**17**
20 Smear human rights NGOs day	**21 MAR HUMAN RIGHTS DAY**	**22** Burgle those pesky judges day	**23** Smear pesky judges day	**2**
27	28	29	30	

22-3-17
DAILY MAVERICK
ZAPIRO

22 March 2017

28 March 2017

He orders the finance minster (and deputy Mcebisi Jonas) back to
SA immediately in the middle of an international investment roadshow

29 March 2017 — The rand plummets amid speculation of a Gupta-driven cabinet reshuffle

78

The president stays away from Ahmed Kathrada's funeral in accordance with the family's wishes. In his eulogy, former president Kgalema Motlanthe quotes the struggle icon's open letter calling on Zuma to stand down.

30 March 2017

Late at night, Zuma proclaims the need for radical economic transformation
and finally axes his finance minister, replacing him not with Brian Molefe,
as many expected, but with another Gupta-linked figure in Malusi Gigaba

2 April 2017

4 April 2017

At last the Guptas have their man in the finance ministry – the previous attempt
with Des van Rooyen in 2015 lasted only 48 hours before protests forced him out

5 April 2017

Just four days after Gordhan's axing, ratings agency Standard & Poor's
downgrades SA's credit to sub-investment levels

6 - 4 - 17 DAILY MAVERICK ZAPIRO ©

6 April 2017

Three of the ANC's top six criticise the reshuffle and
then back down in a National Working Committee meeting

16 April 2017

Equivocation from Gwede Mantashe who now says
Zuma's critics shouldn't have aired their views in public

Over 100 000 attend an anti-Zuma protest at the Union Buildings

11 April 2017   In the past it was Lady Justice in this kind of peril, now it's the entire nation

Dandy new finance minister is off to USA to woo investors while another
controversy brews over the nationalisation dogma of his adviser Prof Chris Malikane

Having missed out on the finance ministry, Brian Molefe gets
big compensation in a massive resignation payout from Eskom

DÉJÀ ZUMA

23 April 2017

Zuma's former wife Nkosazana is very much up and running
for the party presidency. Cover for him from prosecution, perhaps?

It's all a bit late – the deputy president enters the fray, decrying corrupt patronage and demanding a judicial inquiry into state capture

25 April 2017

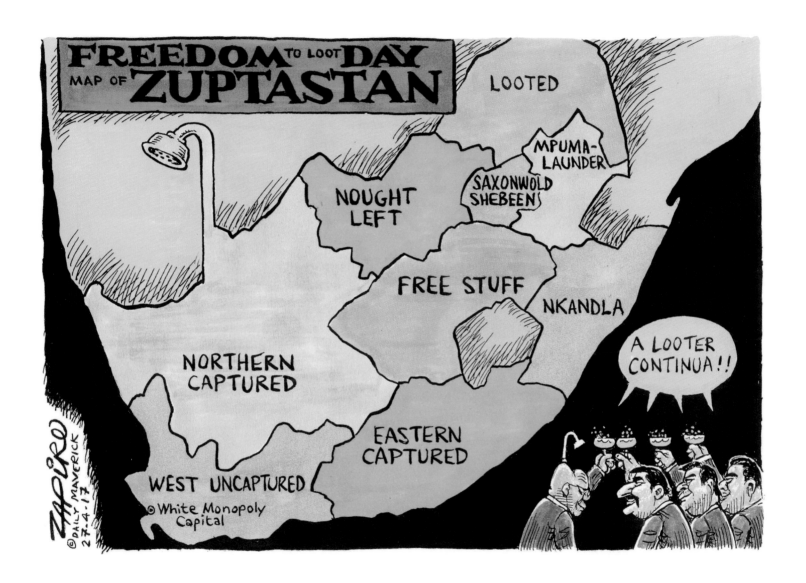

Zuma is booed and prevented from speaking at Cosatu's May Day rally.
Meanwhile, Zwelinzima Vavi addresses newly launched federation
SAFTU as its general secretary and prioritises workers' rights.

30 April 2017

EFF spokesperson is social media's hot new thing

5 May 2017

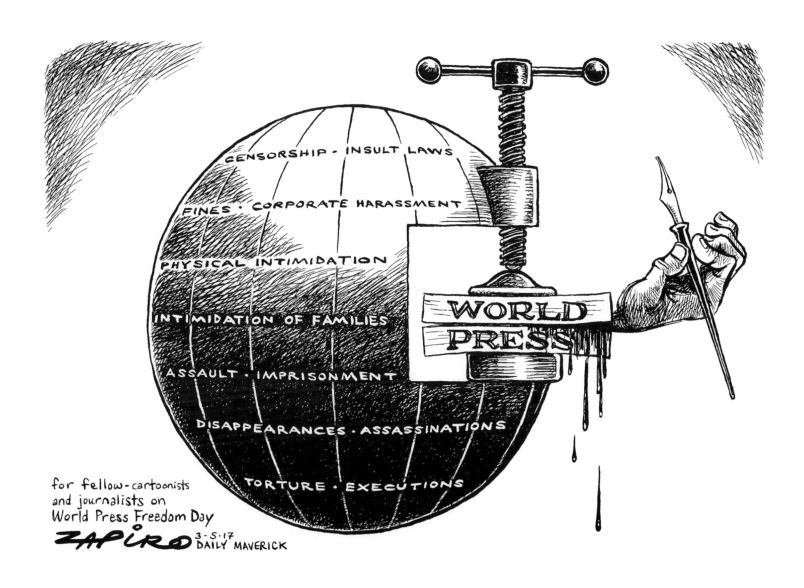

CENSORSHIP · INSULT LAWS

FINES · CORPORATE HARASSMENT

PHYSICAL INTIMIDATION

INTIMIDATION OF FAMILIES

ASSAULT · IMPRISONMENT

DISAPPEARANCES · ASSASSINATIONS

TORTURE · EXECUTIONS

WORLD PRESS

for fellow-cartoonists
and journalists on
World Press Freedom Day
ZAPIRO 3-5-17
DAILY MAVERICK

3 May 2017

Prince Philip retires from public duties

Four wild lions have been on the loose in Mpumalanga.
Molefe is set for a startling return to Eskom where huge contracts are up for grabs.

14 May 2017

16 May 2017

The public enterprises minister approves Molefe's
reappointment but disapproves of the R30m resignation payout

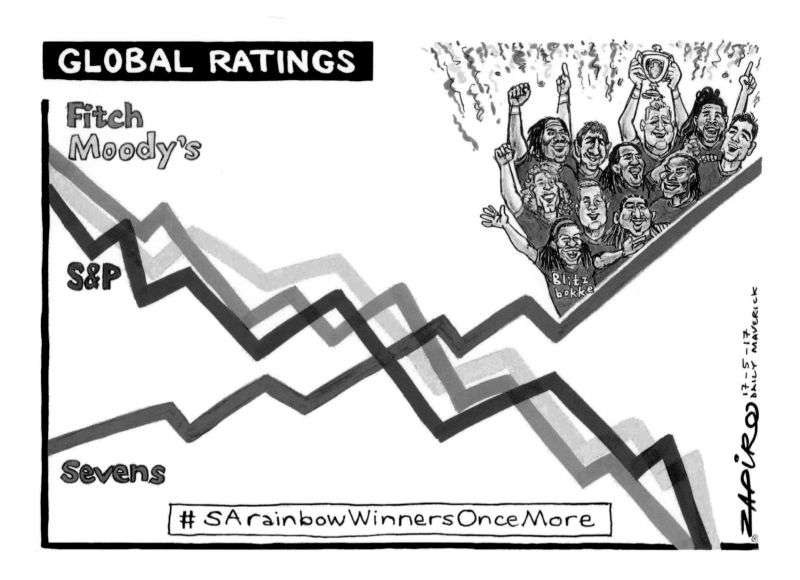

GLOBAL RATINGS

Fitch
Moody's

S&P

Sevens

#SArainbowWinnersOnceMore

Blitz bokke

ZAPIRO 17-5-17 DAILY MAVERICK

17 May 2017

SA rugby sevens team takes world crown in style

19 May 2017

AmaBhungane investigative journalists reveal Brian Molefe and Eskom chair Ben Ngubane pressured a cabinet minister to blackmail mining giant Glencore in favour of the Guptas

NOT The ANC Campaign Race 2017

21 May 2017

23 May 2017

Trump visits Israel for talks with PM Benjamin Netanyahu

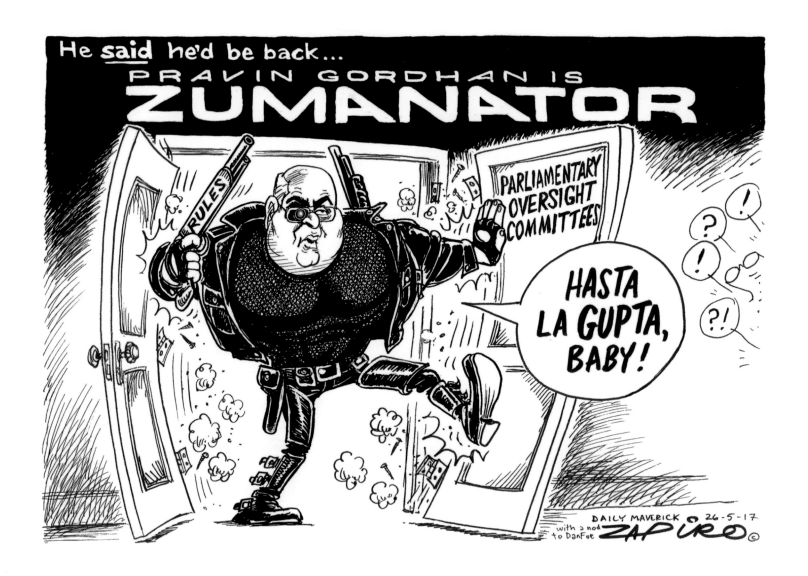

Now an ordinary backbench MP, Gordhan leads
the roasting of the Eskom board and minister Lynne Brown

1 June 2017

CEO of the company involved in the social grants
payment crisis steps down with a massive golden handshake

GUPTA LEAKS

CLICK!

thanks mike w.
4·6·17 SUN. TIMES
ZAPIRO ©

4 June 2017

#GuptaLeaks begin — news media expose a monumental
trove of Gupta e-mails detailing the extent of state capture

Among the first revelations is a scheme for Zuma
and his family to acquire residency in the UAE

The investigation involves a rare collaboration between multiple media networks

8 June 2017

#GuptaLeaks reveal that when finance minister Malusi Gigaba was
public enterprises minister, he'd appointed Gupta associates to key positions in SOEs

7 June 2017

'Storm of the Century' forecast for Cape Town

11 June 2017

Overconfident British prime minister Theresa May is humiliated in a
snap election she called to get a clear mandate on Britain's exit from the EU

13 June 2017   At long last he's fired by the SABC board for misconduct and bringing the organisation into disrepute

14 June 2017

Moody's downgrades ratings for the five largest SA banks

16 June 2017   June 16 — the ANC Youth League has announced support for Nkosazana Dlamini-Zuma

18 June 2017   Noisy protests at his Youth Day speech in North West Province

The Public Protector goes way beyond her powers and calls for a constitutional change
in the Reserve Bank's mandate as part of her investigation into an apartheid-era bank bailout

20 June 2017

23 June 2017

Social media smear campaign against Gupta opponents
traced to 'sockpuppet accounts' emanating from their premises

WILLING BUYER, WILLING SELLER

27 June 2017   The debate on land restoration is reignited

Ahead of another parliamentary motion of no confidence in Zuma,
Chief Justice Mogoeng Mogoeng rules a secret ballot is legal but not obligatory.
Speaker Baleka Mbete must decide rationally and not favour her party.

25 June 2017

119

An infamous apartheid-era security forces' crime is re-examined

30 June 2017

Crucial party meeting gets under way

5 July 2017   … and ends predictably

4 July 2017

#GuptaLeaks reveal that government money indirectly
paid for the infamous Gupta family wedding at Sun City in 2013

7 July 2017

Next #GuptaLeaks allegation – two Gupta brothers sexually harassed their employees

Two British Polluters

SUN.TIMES 9-7-17
thanks Leon G.   ZAPIRO ©

bp
POLLUTING THE ENVIRONMENT

Bell Pottinger
POLLUTING THE MIND

Victoria Geoghegan

SMEAR BOTS
POISON POLIT
Gupta lies
fake sites
RACE HATRED
toxic tweets
race baiting

SA

9 July 2017

Now #GuptaLeaks expose the dirty tricks of the London-based
PR agency working for a company owned by the brothers

Leader of the Free World

11 July 2017

Hosting the G20 Hamburg summit, German chancellor
Angela Merkel has more than just global issues to deal with

The latest of many curious break-ins. Documents and laptops are stolen from the NPA offices of the team investigating a senior Hawks officer for kidnapping.

12 July 2017

16 July 2017

Leaked e-mail woes — their taxes and state contracts are scrutinised,
banks close their accounts, major firms dealing with them are slammed …

WHERE IS SHAUN?

WHERE IS SHAUN?

WHERE IS SHAUN?

WHERE IS SHAUN?

WHERE IS SHAUN?!

WHERE THE F*** IS SHAUN?!!

Multitude of potentially criminal acts revealed in #GuptaLeaks,
zero response from NPA boss Shaun Abrahams

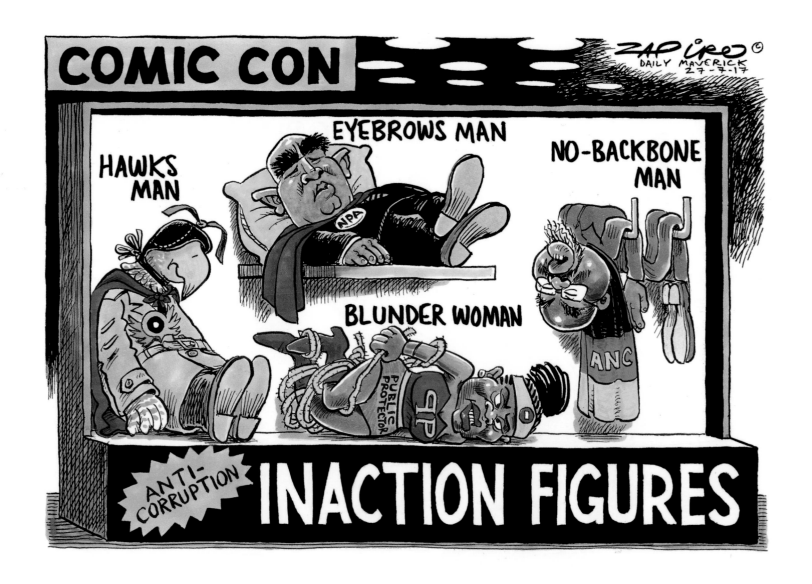

27 July 2017

It will be the eighth such parliamentary no-confidence motion
but this time some ANC MPs are publicly breaking ranks

1 August 2017

6 August 2017

8 August 2017

Speculation mounts that he might lose

9 August 2017 Despite significant defections, he survives once again

2 August 2017   Not for the first time, one of North Korea's many missile tests goes haywire

Deputy minister Mduduzi Manana is caught on camera assaulting two women
at a Jo'burg nightclub. ANC Women's League president Bathabile Dlamini is unfazed.

10 August 2017

13 August 2017

Long-awaited freedom for a South African
motorbiking tourist taken by al-Qaeda in Timbuktu

15 August 2017

SA athletics stars shine at the world champs in London

In Jo'burg, Zimbabwe's first lady finds her sons in the company of a woman whom she brutally whips with an extension cord. Now she wants diplomatic immunity from international relations minister Maite Nkoana-Mashabane.

16 August 2017

The ANC lambastes Makhosi Khoza for voting against Zuma
in parliament and axes her as a committee chairperson

Marikana miners killed by police on 16 Aug. 2012:	Number of their dependants:	Days since the massacre:	Number of people who know the real story through award-winning media:	Price paid by one Lonmin director in 2012 for a buffalo: *	Compensation paid to families:	Police / Lonmin execs/ politicians/ facing charges:
34	±300	1826	HUNDREDS OF THOUSANDS	R13 MILLION	0	0

MINERS SHOT DOWN
REHAD DESAI

GREG MARINOVICH
MURDER AT SMALL KOPPIE
THE REAL STORY OF THE MARIKANA MASSACRE

DAILY MAVERICK
Marikana: official lies, cover-up

(* actual purchase, not the failed R18 mill. bid)

CR

DAILY MAVERICK 16 Aug 2017
ZAPIRO

25 August 2017

Marikana community and unionists chase away
ANC presidential candidate Nkosazana Dlamini-Zuma

The Guptas sell their media assets at inflated values to mouthpiece
Mzwanele Manyi – and they lend him the money for the deal

22 August 2017

27 August 2017

The finance minister wants government to sell its stake in
Telkom to fund yet another huge bailout for the national carrier

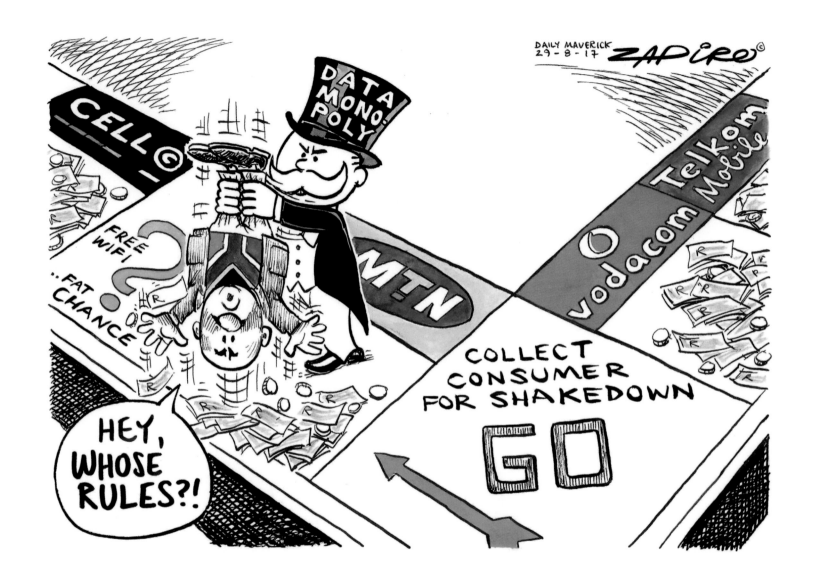

29 August 2017

The Competition Commission is investigating
SA data prices which are among the world's highest

30 August 2017

Intrepid head of the Independent Police Investigative Directorate is in personal trouble again. This time, Robert McBride faces claim he assaulted his teenage daughter.

1 September 2017

On tax deadline day, the latest #GuptaLeaks exposé suggests the Guptas persuaded SARS that they earned less than R1 million in each of the past three years

3 September 2017

The president's most captured son gives a rare interview in Dubai

Latest in the ANC presidential candidacy dirty-tricks saga:
Ramaphosa attempts to clear his name after front-page newspaper leaks
of personal e-mails detailing alleged affairs with a number of women

5 September 2017

151

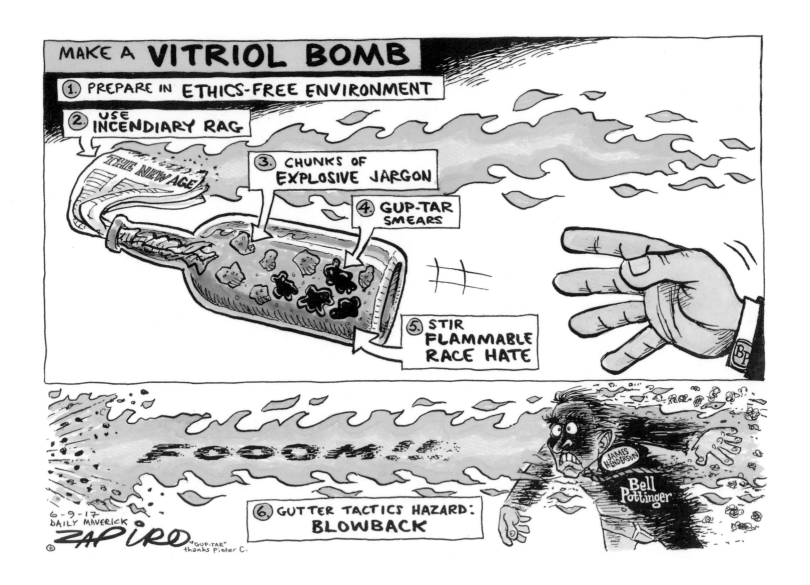

6 September 2017

UK Public Relations and Communications Council terminates the membership of Bell Pottinger because of unethical behaviour in their work for the Guptas. Chief executive James Henderson soon resigns.

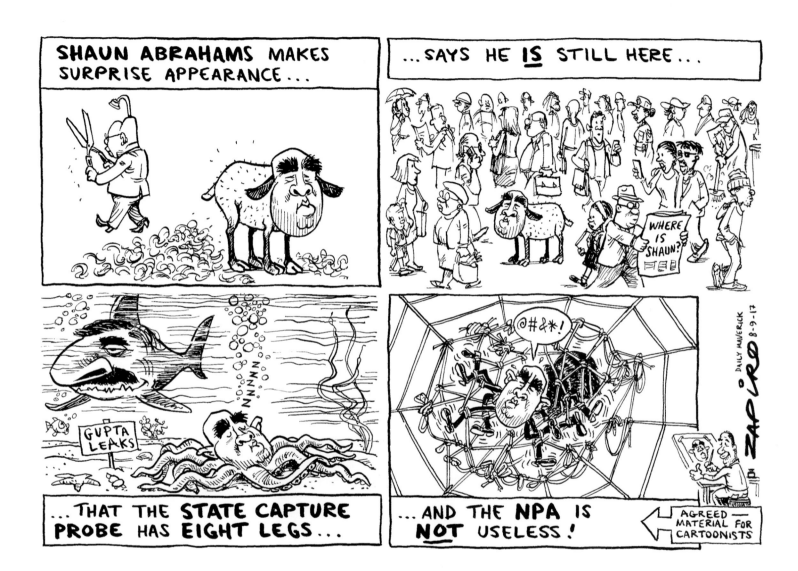

Stuart Baxter's woeful Bafana Bafana lose two World Cup qualifiers
to minnows Cape Verde, then FIFA orders a replay of a rare
earlier win over Senegal because the ref was palpably bent

10 September 2017

Nobel Peace Prize winner and global icon ignores the desperate plight
of Myanmar's Rohingya people. Hundreds have been killed
by military forces and over 300 000 have fled.

13 September 2017

12 September 2017   40th anniversary of the death in police custody of Black Consciousness icon

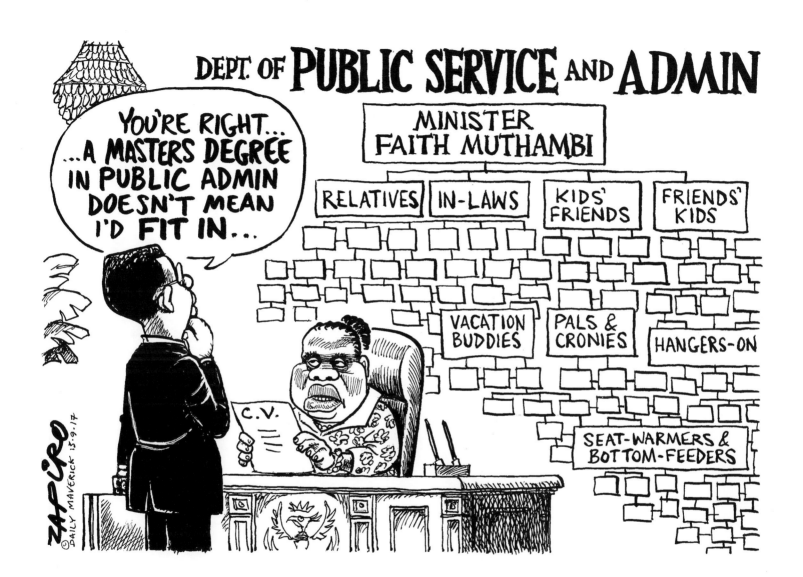

Faith Muthambi tells parliament she employed nine relatives in her
department and flew 30 people to her budget speech at taxpayers' expense
and believes it's all in accordance with the ministerial handbook

15 September 2017

17 September 2017

It's taken nine years. In the Supreme Court his lawyers admit that
the NPA's dropping of 783 corruption charges against him was irrational.

THE GUPTA EFFECT...

DAILY MAVERICK 19-9-17 ZAPIRO

Top firm's leadership resigns with grovelling apology and a promise
to pay back fees earned from auditing dubious Gupta deals and
producing the discredited SARS report used to target Pravin Gordhan

19 September 2017

21 September 2017